TOP DOGS

Boxer

Charles and Linda George

Created by Q2AMedia
www.q2amedia.com
Editor Jeff O' Hare
Publishing Director Chester Fisher
Client Service Manager Santosh Vasudevan
Project Manager Kunal Mehrotra
Art Director Harleen Mehta
Designer Pragati Gupta
Picture Researcher Nivisha Sinha

Library of Congress Cataloging-in-Publication Data
Boxer / [Charles George,Linda George].
p. cm. — (Top dogs)
Includes index.
ISBN 0-531-23240-9/ 978-0-531-23240-8 (hardcover)
1. Boxer (Dog breed)—Juvenile literature. I. Title. II. Series.
SF429.B75B627 2010
636.73—dc22
2010035029

This edition published by Scholastic Inc.,

Printed and bound in Heshan, China
232658 10/10
10 9 8 7 6 5 4 3 2 1

Picture Credits
t= top, b= bottom, c= center, r= right, l= left

Cover Page: Andrey.Tiyk/Shutterstock, Uan Silva/Istockphoto.

Title Page: Mars Evis/Shutterstock.

4-5: Karen Givens/Shutterstock; 5: Adamgolabek/Fotolia; 6-7: K.U. Habler/Fotolia;
7: Morgan Lane Photography/Shutterstock; 8-9: Vyacheslav Anyakin/Dreamstime;
9: Erika Walsh/Fotolia; 10-11: Bonzami Emmanuelle/123RF; 12-13: Cynoclub/Fotolia;
13: Carmen Martinez Banus/Istockphoto; 14: K.U. Habler/Fotolia; 15: Inacio Pires/Dreamstime;
16: Emmanuelle Bonzami/Bigstock; 17: Andrea Biraghi/123RF; 18: Genadi Yakovlev/
Dreamstime; 18-19: Janno/Shutterstock; 19: Stana/Fotolia; 20: Jose Gil/Istockphoto;
21: Aleksei Frolkov/Dreamstime; 22: Louise Avila/Photolibrary; 23: Jason Kennedy/Fotolia;
24-25: Sonya Etchison/Dreamstime; 26-27: Dennis Kleiman/Getty Images; 28: Frank Siteman/
Photolibrary; 29: Marc O'Sullivan/Rex Features; 30-31: J-L. Klein & M-L. Hubert/Photolibrary.

Contents

What are Boxers?

Boxers came to the U.S. from Germany. They were used for hunting larger animals. They were sent to find an animal that had been shot by a hunter. The boxer held onto the animal until the hunter found them.

Fast Fact

Boxers came from a breed of dogs that is now **extinct**.

No one is sure why these dogs are called boxers. Some say it's because the dogs tend to use their front paws when they fight, just like human boxers. Others say it is because of their box-shaped heads.

We Love Boxers!

Many people love boxers, but they aren't the right dog for everyone. They **mature** slowly. They act like puppies most of their lives. After they reach the age of three or four, they calm down a little.

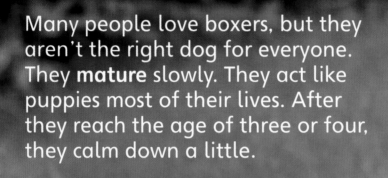

Fast Fact

Boxers are the clowns of the dog world. They enjoy acting silly!

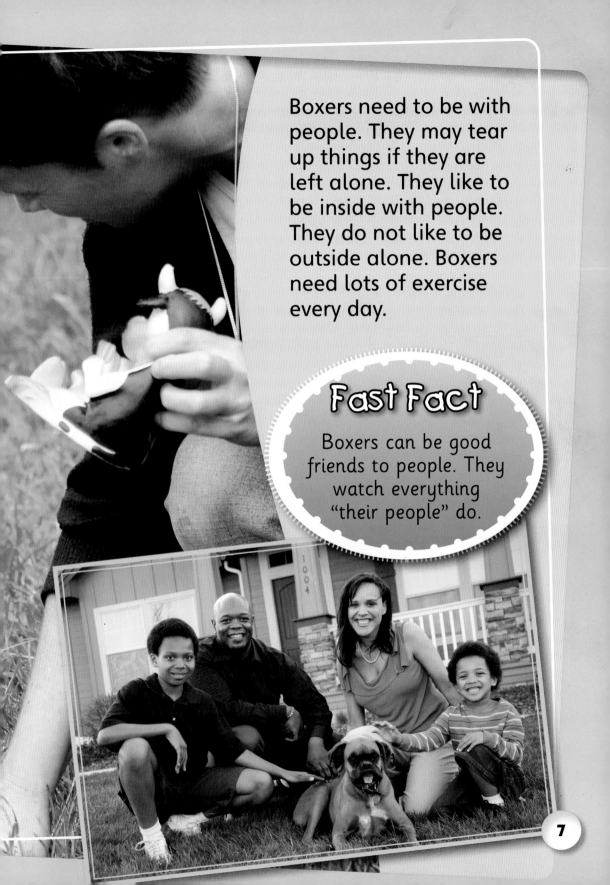

Boxers need to be with people. They may tear up things if they are left alone. They like to be inside with people. They do not like to be outside alone. Boxers need lots of exercise every day.

Fast Fact

Boxers can be good friends to people. They watch everything "their people" do.

Boxers Love Kids!

Fast Fact

Be gentle when playing with any dog. A dog will nip or growl if you are not good to it.

Most boxers like children. They will **protect** the children they know. Boxers do not get easily upset if they are poked by children. Most of the time, they enjoy children petting them.

Boxers enjoy playing. Sometimes they can be silly! Many children like watching boxer puppies jump around. Boxers like hearing children laugh! They want to laugh, too!

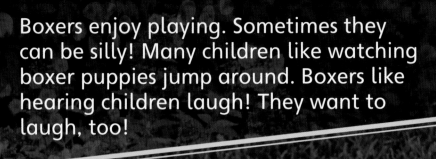

Fast Fact

Perhaps boxers get along so well with children because they are kids at heart. They enjoy doing childlike things.

Baby Boxers

A boxer puppy weighs about 11-15 ounces (0.3-0.4 kg) when it is born. Start teaching your boxer puppy as soon as it's **weaned** from its mother's milk. This happens when the dog is about six weeks old.

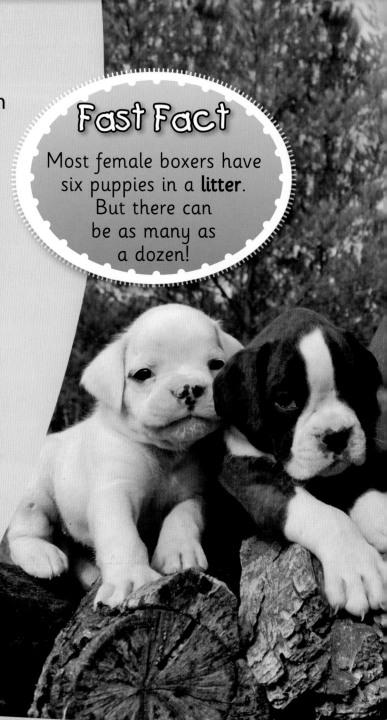

Fast Fact

Most female boxers have six puppies in a **litter**. But there can be as many as a dozen!

Your family must teach the boxer puppy how to behave. Teaching your puppy will take a lot of **patience**. You may have to teach the same lessons over and over.

Fast Fact

Boxer puppies like to **explore**. You must teach them not to jump, chew, or dig in the house.

Choosing a Boxer Puppy

A male boxer is more playful than a female. Try to find a dog that's right for your family. If your family likes being outside and active, choose an active puppy. If your family likes being inside, choose a quieter puppy.

Fast Fact

Don't choose a boxer if you can't spend a lot of time with it.

Fast Fact

When choosing a puppy, pick one that has plenty of energy. Make sure it gets along well with its brothers and sisters, too.

Boxer puppies like to explore. They like sniffing at all sorts of things. Boxers can't stand to be cold. Be sure they have a warm place to stay.

Taking Care of Your Boxer Puppy

Fast Fact

Take your puppy to meet other people and dogs. This will help it learn to be friendly.

A boxer puppy needs time to get used to people. Gently put your puppy on its back. Playfully roll it from side to side. Touch its feet. Brush it gently. Pet it several times a day. All this will help your puppy get used to your touch.

Fast Fact

Boxers hate getting wet! Keep this in mind when it's time for your puppy's first bath.

A boxer puppy should be checked by a veterinarian from time to time. A veterinarian, also called a vet, is a doctor just for animals. Your vet will tell you if your new puppy is healthy. The vet will also give your puppy its shots, to keep it healthy.

How Big Do Boxers Get?

Boxers are medium-sized dogs. Male boxers stand between 23-25 inches (57-63 cm) tall. They weigh about 66-70 pounds (30-32 kg). Females stand about 21-23 inches (53-59 cm) tall. They weigh about 55-60 pounds (25-27 kg).

Fast Fact

Like all dogs, you should teach boxers when they are young. Boxers are harder to teach when they get older.

Boxers love to play, but they may play too rough. You should be careful when playing with your boxer. They have strong muscles. Most of the time, they want to roll, jump around, and run. They might knock you down!

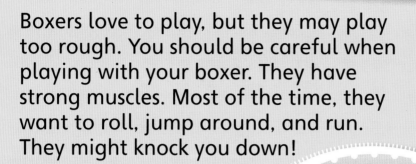

Fast Fact

Boxers are mostly friendly, but they will protect their family.

Brushing Hair and Clipping Nails

Boxers have short hair. Their hair can be brindle, fawn, or white. Fawn is a light shade of brown. Brindle generally means several colors mixed together with black marks.

Fast Fact

White patches on a brindle or fawn boxer are called "flashes." Some boxers have no flashes. Others may have big ones.

Brushing keeps a boxer from **shedding** too much hair. Your pet's doctor should keep its nails short.

Fast Fact

A boxer with only white hair is called "ultra flashy." You'll never see a boxer with only black hair.

Make Room for Your Boxer!

Boxers are mainly house dogs. They do well in most indoor spaces. They should get exercise every day. It's best not to leave them outside. They may get sick if they get too hot or too cold.

Fast Fact

Take your boxer to a large yard or dog park where it can run. Teach your boxer to come when you call its name.

Boxers like having their own beds. They also like sleeping near their people at night. It is best if they don't sleep on your bed. They **drool!** And, sometimes, they snore!

Fast Fact

Boxers have been known to jump over a six-foot (1.8-m) fence if they are left alone.

Sweet Boxers

Fast Fact

Boxers get along with other pets in the house— even cats!

Boxers are loving dogs. As much as they enjoy playing, they also like to curl up for a nap next to you. Like most dogs, they love being petted.

Fast Fact

Boxers have strong jaws and lots of energy. They really like playing tug-of-war.

A boxer wants your attention. It will love when you talk to it or pet it. Be sure your boxer has toys to play with if you have to leave it alone.

Curious About Everything!

Boxers enjoy learning new things. They love to go on walks and runs. They can smell if animals have been in the area. When they pick up a **scent**, they want to find the animal.

Fast Fact

Boxers want to know what's behind every bush, under every log, or around every corner.

Fast Fact

Boxers are very strong. Have an adult hold the leash when you walk your dog.

Use a **harness** instead of a collar when walking your boxer on a **leash**. Your boxer may pull hard when it wants to check something out. A harness won't choke your dog when it wants to go faster than you!

Loyal Friends

Boxers protect the people they love. Sometimes, they bark too much, even after being told to stop. They are telling you to be careful. Boxers should never be treated only as dogs that protect. They want to be part of the family.

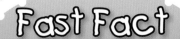

Fast Fact

Female boxers can be very forceful when they are trying to protect someone.

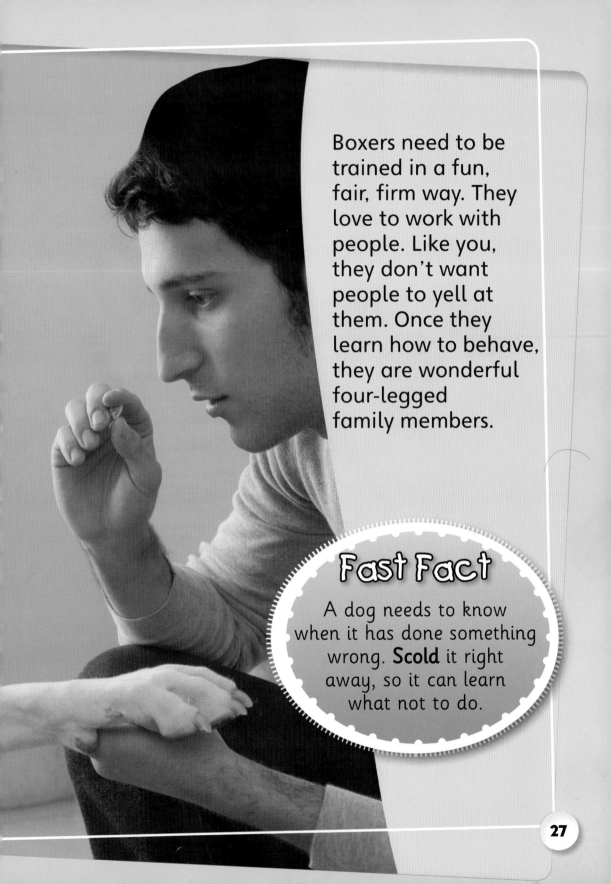

Boxers need to be trained in a fun, fair, firm way. They love to work with people. Like you, they don't want people to yell at them. Once they learn how to behave, they are wonderful four-legged family members.

Fast Fact

A dog needs to know when it has done something wrong. **Scold** it right away, so it can learn what not to do.

Boxers Helping People

Fast Fact

Petting a boxer makes people feel better. That's good therapy for the people and also for the dog!

Boxers make great family pets. They are also sometimes used as police dogs, **guide dogs**, and **herding dogs**. They also make good **therapy dogs**. Therapy dogs visit people who are sick or who live alone.

Boxers make good dogs for people who can't hear. Boxers will let their owners know when the phone rings, when the doorbell sounds, or when an alarm goes off.

Fast Fact

Many celebrities own boxers, including Robin Williams, Jennifer Love Hewitt, and George Clooney.

A long time ago, boxers were used by **soldiers** to carry messages. Boxers also helped protect **soldiers.** The dogs listened for **enemy** soldiers and barked to warn their owners.

Fast Fact

Boxers always protect their owners. They bark when they feel danger is near.

Punch and Judy were two boxers who were with British soldiers in Israel in 1946. They heard enemies trying to sneak up on the soldiers. Punch and Judy barked and warned their owners. They saved the soldiers' lives.

Fast Fact

Punch and Judy were each given an award for saving two British soldiers.

Glossary

Drool – slobber; spit that falls out of the mouth

Enemy – person on the other team, someone who is against you

Explore – look for new things

Extinct – no longer living

Guide dogs – dogs trained to help people who can't see

Harness – straps that go around a dog's chest and neck

Herding dogs – dogs trained to work with cattle, goats, or other farm animals, to keep them together or to make them go somewhere

Leash – a strap that is attached to a collar or harness, to help control a dog on a walk

Litter – a group of puppies born to one mother, all at one time

Mature – to grow up or grown-up

Patience – being able to wait

Scent – a smell

Scold – talk in an angry voice

Shed – to lose hair

Soldiers – people serving in the military

Therapy dogs – dogs trained to visit sick people or people who live alone

Weaned – stopped from drinking mother's milk and made to eat other food

Index